NO FAIL GUITAR

A Proven Four-Step System That Lets Any Beginner
Learn To Play Real Songs.

BGS

BECKWITH
GUITAR SYSTEMS

Published by: Beckwith Guitar Systems

NO FAIL GUITAR:

A Proven Four-Step System That Let's Any Beginner Learn to Play Real Songs

BGS

BECKWITH
GUITAR SYSTEMS

Published by: Beckwith Guitar Systems

PO Box 426
2300 Williams Blvd.
Kenner, La 70062-9998

www.beguitarsys.com

copyright © James Beckwith 2011

ISBN # 978-0-9830298-1-6

Cover Design: Katherine Klimitas
Book Design: Katherine Klimitas and James Beckwith

Neither the author or publisher are responsible for any errors or omissions. Inclusion in this book does not constitute an endorsement by the author or publisher unless stated otherwise.

WARNING! This book was not written by an English major. Grammatical and punctuatuation errors are present. Proceed with caution.

Acknowledgements:

To my students, for making me think! The Klimitas family, for their hospitality and expertise. West Warren, for the use of an awesome guitar. And finally, to my mom, Winelle Beckwith, for her encouragement and support. Thanks to all!

In Memory of My Father, Gene H. Beckwith

TABLE OF CONTENTS

TRACK LIST

Download Code: **bgsmusic**

INTRODUCTION
Even You Can Play Guitar!

There are many books out there that seem to promise the impossible, ("Learn to play instantly, even if you're an idiot!"). I'm glad you picked up this one, and my promise is a little more modest:

Everyone Can Play Guitar!

Yes, even you. Maybe you've tried before, even gotten a few books or videos, but somehow couldn't put it all together. I've been teaching for over twenty-five years, and I've taught thousands to play the guitar. Male and female, ages six to seventy, and if they can do it, so can you!

This book addresses the most common problem I see, and it's not lack of information! If anything, there's too much information that is pointless and leaves the beginner confused and discouraged. The problem for most people is putting chords together and *strumming non-stop*. The good news is, you don't need a four hundred-page book with hundreds of pictures and diagrams to do this!

What you need is a system. A system that boils down all the endless advice and diagrams to a few essentials to remember and tackles the main problem, how to move both hands together and play the guitar!

This Is Why My Book Is Different!

My system is different because it's short and to the point. Over the years I have peeled away the unnecessary stuff and kept the basics, until I was left with a simple system that seemed to work for anybody that wanted to become a decent guitarist within a short time. By decent guitar I mean strumming songs so your family and friends can recognize them. By short time I mean playing your first song in a few weeks and the basic idea in three to six months. By that time, you should be able to play and understand a simple chord chart from sheet music and play six to twelve actual songs. Most important, you will be able to locate and learn to play the kind of music you like...real songs!

How This Book Is Organized.

I've organized this book as follows:

- Chapter 1 answers briefly the six most common questions I get from new students.

- Chapter 2 presents the **learning template,** my system for you to teach yourself how to move both hands together and play the guitar. This is the core of the book.

- Chapters 3-8 demonstrate my method using actual songs and chord progressions. As you can see from the table of contents, this book is written mainly for adults. The songs are "classic rock", blues and folk songs good for strumming with family, friends, church etc. While the songs are easier to learn in this sequence you don't have to, each song stands on its' own.

- Chapter 9 expands this system to other sources of music; song books, internet, church music and more. This will enable you to learn what you want.

- Chapter 10 is the appendix. It's basically a collection of short answers to various questions you might have on equipment, chords, strums, etc. Since I don't know your level of knowledge, and I didn't want to clutter up the book with endless explanations and re-hashings, I just put the "nuts & bolts" in the last chapter. All bolded terms throughout the book can be found here with more explanation. You can refer to it if you need it.

A final feature will be...

Chapter Summaries (like this one):

Introduction Summary:

- This book is for adult beginners. (not kids, headbangers, or lead guitarists).

- This book tackles the main problem beginners face; *how to move both hands together and play guitar!*

- You should start playing your first song in a few weeks, and get the basic idea in three to six months.

- This book is short!

If you've tried to play guitar before and were frustrated because you couldn't get the hang of it, give my system a try. It's short, simple, and most important, proven with *thousands of students!*

CHAPTER ONE

The Big Six

QUESTIONS?

CHECK THE
APPENDIX!

This chapter answers the six questions I get asked most often by new students when we first meet or talk on the phone.

- *What will I learn?*

- *Will I learn to read music?*

- *How long will it take?*

- *How much practice will I need?*

- *What if I'm left-handed?*

- *What type of guitar should I get? Where?*

I'm keeping the answers brief in this chapter, you can find more information in the **appendix.**

1. What Will I Learn?

In order to play decent rhythm guitar (strumming chords), you will need to know:

- 12 to 18 chords

- 4 to 6 strum patterns

- How to tune your guitar

   You will learn all of this by learning to play the songs and progressions given in chapters three through eight. There are no exercises in this report. The songs *are* the exercise. The reason the number of chords and strums varies depends on the style(s) of music you want to play.

2. Will I Learn To Read Music?

No, not in this book. While music notation can be helpful, and is necessary for classical, jazz, and professionals, that's not our goal. You will learn to read a **chord chart** and some basic **rhythm notation.** You will also learn to read **tablature,** an extremely easy way to read guitar music.

3. How Long Will It Take?

Everybody's situation is different obviously, but over the years I've found about three to six months for the basic stuff outlined in question one. This depends on the amount of practice, talent, self-confidence, etc. You should be able to play your first song by one month, and at least six more after six months. Depending on how you define "songs", you could be playing hundreds! (A lot of folk tunes and 50's tunes are pretty simple.)

4. How Much Should I Practice?

Not much, about twenty minutes a day, five or six days a week should do it. It's more important to develop the habit of daily practice. Twenty minutes a day six days a week is way better than two hours all in one day. You are building a physical reflex, not cramming for a test, cramming won't work. Give yourself a day off too; six days is enough.

5. What If I'm Left-Handed?

If you are a complete beginner, I would learn to play right-handed. After all, you have to use both hands to play, and the left hand does most of the work. Left-handed guitars are also harder to find and cost a little more. If you already have a left-handed guitar or you just can't stand the idea of playing right-handed, go ahead and learn left-handed. Since this book is for right-handed people, you will need to reverse the pictures, so please go slow and pay attention to string and fret numbers.

6. What Type Of Guitar Should I Get? Where?

I'll tackle the second question first, **where do I buy a guitar?** A beginner should buy at a local music store. While mail-order, pawn shops and big box stores can be cheaper, they won't help you if your guitar breaks or show you how to use your tuner.

A good store should find time to talk with you if they aren't busy. If they won't talk to you, find another store. The only two exceptions to this rule are if you have an experienced friend to help you, or if you live in an area with no music stores. In that case, mail-order/internet is your main option. I'll have suggestions for that in the appendix.

What type of guitar should I buy? Don't spend a lot! I recommend an *inexpensive guitar*; good enough to stay in tune, easy to play, and last for a year or more (maybe forever) until you outgrow it. You should get a decent guitar for $100 to $300, anything much below $100 is likely to be a toy.*

- **acoustic guitars:** Also called box guitars, this is the way to go if your budget is tight. You can buy a decent guitar for as little as $100, although $150 is more likely, plus about $20 for a soft case. I would go for steel strings instead of nylon (see appendix for more info).

- **electric guitars:** It's what the kids want, and a lot of adults too. A decent electric guitar runs about the same as an acoustic, $100 to $200, but you also need an amplifier and connecting cable, which can add another $150. You can often purchase a guitar/amp package for $200 to $300, which includes guitar, amplifier, case, and cable (ask and make sure it *does*).

I have included more information on shopping, brands, strings, and maintenance in the equipment section located in the appendix. If you need more information, look there!

Chapter One Summary:

You will need:

- 12 to 18 chords, plus a few strums and tuning. (And no music reading!)

- About 20 minutes a day, six days a week for 3 to 6 months. You should be strumming a song in about a month.

- $100 to $300 depending on your guitar preference. (And it's more affordable to play right-handed.)

Now that you have your guitar it's time to begin. The next chapter, The Learning Template, tackles what I consider to be the main challenge of learning to play guitar, *moving both hands together and switching chords*. Over the years I have found this system to be the fastest way to get results on the guitar, and I'm confident it will work for you!

*These are 2010 prices.

CHAPTER TWO
The Learning Template

QUESTIONS?

CHECK THE
APPENDIX!

The word *template* is defined as a pattern or guide used to make something. In this case our template is a four-step learning process I use to enable beginners to play a song. (What we're making is a guitar player!) As I stated in the introduction, the problem for most people is putting the chords together and *strumming non-stop.* I can't begin to describe how many times I've seen a student carefully arrange their fingers into a chord, start strumming and then *stop,* carefully re-arrange their fingers into the next chord and continue strumming. Does this sound familiar? If you've tried to play before without success, I bet it does. So how do we solve this problem? I'm glad you asked! We solve it by using the main principle I've learned in over twenty-five years of teaching guitar. Here it is:

You can learn anything, if you take it in small bits and go slow.

For the beginner, this means *don't try to learn both hands at the same time!* Yes it takes two hands to play the guitar, but that doesn't mean you should learn it that way. Can *you* learn two different things at the same time? *I* can't. Learn each hand separately and *then* put them together. This is the idea behind my LEARNING TEMPLATE, composed of four easy steps.

THE LEARNING TEMPLATE:

1. Learn the chords and decide on a *finger sequence.*

2. Using the *EZ Strum* and *finger sequence,* practice switching chords while strumming non-stop.

3. Learn the appropriate *Basic strum pattern,* and practice strumming with one chord.

4. Combine the two hands.

The rest of this chapter, a whopping three pages, is devoted to explaining this outline. Please do not skip this, as it is the core of what I teach and you will refer back to it as you learn the songs in this book, or any other song for that matter. *So please read!*

Before we begin, there is an important point to keep in mind; *pick an easy song!*

It may seem obvious, but your first song (probably your first dozen songs), should be easy! I've picked six for this book and listed a lot more to try in the back. What do I mean by easy? An easy song should have four to five chords max, most of which you recognize, and not be too fast or complicated. While some of the songs I picked may not be exactly what you like, you should find a few that are close. Just learn these and later on I will tell you how to locate and play whatever it is you want. Also, try and obtain a recorded copy of the song you are learning. It will come in handy as a reference to help you learn, and it's fun to play along with! Now that you've picked an easy song, let's go over the four steps:

1. Learn The Chords And Decide On A *Finger Sequence.*

Your easy song will contain two to five chords*. For each chord in this book you will see a picture and a diagram, plus a few tips on how to make it. You can also hear what the chord sounds like on the CD. Just practice making the chords until they sound clear and mostly buzz free. Memorize them! If you have to look at the book to remember a chord, it's too late. Learn those suckers! Next, decide on a **finger sequence.** You should always have a finger sequence when you change to a new chord. Instead of trying to move all your fingers at once, pick one finger (always the same one), and move *just that finger* to the right spot for that chord. It's hard to think about a whole chord but it's easy to think about just one finger, so do that! Once that finger is in place, *then* add the remaining fingers one at a time, until you have the chord; (1,2,3 if it's a 3 finger chord). You can practice this without strumming. Remember, when you change chords just think of one finger, *always* practice your chords by putting down one finger at a time. The pictures below show this process with a D chord.

Track #12
D Chord Played
With Finger
Sequence

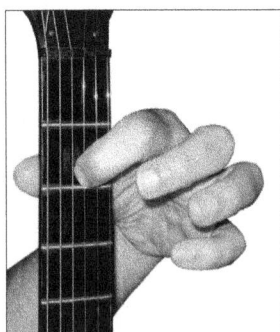

| First Finger D | Second Finger D | D Chord (Third Finger) |

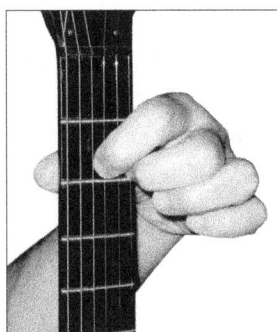

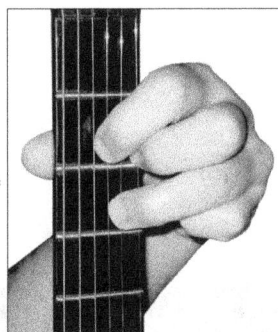

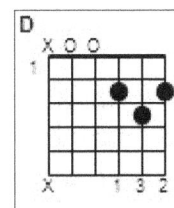

D
X O O

Finger Sequence:
1,2,3.

CD Track #12

*A chord means you strum three or more notes together.

2. Learn And Use The EZ Strum, Then Practice Switching Chords Non-Stop.

The EZ strum is the second key to this whole project. I call it the EZ strum because it only requires about three functioning brain cells to play. Hopefully, you qualify. So here goes; take the pick in your right hand and strum downwards on the strings, not too hard. You don't have to be perfect, just hit most of the strings.

Now do this reasonably steady; blong, blong, blong...Think of your right hand as a machine you turn on and it starts strumming. Don't even look at your right hand, just keep strumming; blong, blong, blong... See? Isn't that easy? Doesn't it sound awful with no chord? So pick the first of those two to five chords you just learned and arrange your fingers (1,2,3!) on it, and *now* practice your EZ strum. Focus all your attention on your chord hand (the left one). Don't even *look* at your right hand, just keep blonging away. *That* is why I call it the EZ strum!

Track #23
EZ Strum
(G Chord)

Now for the biggie, learning to strum & switch chords non-stop. To do this, just apply the main principal; *take it in small bits and go slow!* You can do this by;

- Taking each chord change separately.
- Switching one finger at a time (finger sequence)
- Using the EZ strum and not stopping!

Here is an example:

Track #1 (A)
EZ Strum

Take each chord change separately.

Look at this as a series of small tasks, not one big one. Practice switching from D to A *only*, until you get that down. Then practice from A to G, and finally from G to D. Tackle one change per twenty-minute practice session.

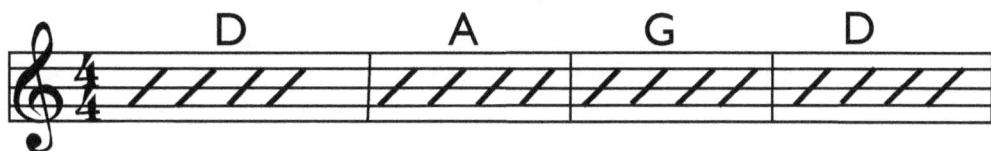

A Chord

Finger Sequence:
1, 2, 3.

CD Track #16

G Chord

Finger Sequence:
3,2,1.

CD Track #14

Switch one finger at a time.

Slowly make a D chord, and then practice moving to an A chord one finger at a time; 1, then 2 and 3. Remember, when you first switch, think of one finger! (then add the rest) You don't have to strum for this step, focus all your attention on your chord hand. When you have this step down, it's time for the last step;

Don't stop strumming!

Now comes the challenge: Arrange your fingers on the D chord. Start the EZ strum and focus your attention on the left hand (chord hand). Keep strumming and switch to the A chord one finger at a time, without stopping the strum! Even if it sounds cheesy and takes ten strums to get your fingers down, keep strumming that EZ strum and switch those fingers! (Your guitar won't blow up, I promise.) Once you're comfortable switching your fingers without stopping the strum, you can start reducing the number of strums it takes to switch. Your goal is to get all fingers down in three or four strums. Whew! Now that you can switch from D to A in three or four strums, without stopping, you're through for the day. Tomorrow you can try A to G, and the day after G to D, etc. Then practice putting them all together for a couple of days, get the idea? Small bits and slow & steady does it, all in twenty minutes a day! Ultimately, you'll want to get all of your fingers down in one strum, that will happen after several weeks of practice. Just keep following the main principle and take it in small steps. Once you can switch chords in four beats, go for three beats, the two beats, until you can switch chords in one beat.

3. Learn The *Basic Strum Pattern,* And Practice With One Chord.

Most sheet music or tabs won't give you a specific strum. You need a collection of basic strum patterns so you can pick the best one and play it. Professionals will vary their strum patterns, depending on their musical interpretation. Since you are just starting, you will want to stick to the basic pattern. You have plenty to think about, so learn the song with the basic strum pattern first, you can mess around with it later, when you're more comfortable playing it. It helps if you can read at least a little **rhythm notation,** and you will have an example on the CD to listen to.

While I generally give these strums a name, (medium 4 for instance), these names are just what *I* call them. If they're referred to at all in sheet music, they are written in rhythm notation. Anyway, learn and listen to the strum for your song and practice it on *one chord only.* Pick the easiest! Focus on your strumming hand and get that right for now, switching chords and strumming comes next! I have chosen the strum pattern I call Medium 4 for the example shown below.

Track #24
Medium 4 Strum
(G Chord)

4. Combine The Two Hands.

The final step is to add the basic strum pattern to the song part you just learned with the EZ strum in step 2. Use the same three steps;

- Take each chord change separately

- Switch one finger at a time.

- Don't stop strumming! (just substitute the medium 4 strum for the EZ strum)

Track #1 (B)
Medium 4 Strum

Remember to *go slow* and *don't stop!* How slow? Slow enough to do it without stopping! You can't play it fast if you can't play it slow, so go slow and *play it!* Then you can speed it up and push yourself to play along with the recording.

Chapter Two Summary:

Pick easy songs, and go slow! Split your task into small bits.

Don't learn two things at once! Start with your

- **Left Hand:** memorize your chords, choose a finger sequence (put them down one at a time), and use the EZ strum so you can focus on your left hand while you learn to change chords *without stopping the strum.* Take one chord change at a time.

- **Right Hand:** choose the best basic strum for your song and practice that with one chord, so you can focus on your right hand while you get the strum pattern down.

Finally...

- Combine both hands and switch chords using the basic strum.

Start with a few of the easy songs in this report, and within a few weeks or months you should be able to branch out and learn what you want. The four part learning template teaches you how to learn!

Bad Moon Rising
Words and Music by John Fogerty

Verse

I see a bad moon a ris - in'. I see

trou-ble on the way. I see earth - quakes and light-

- nin'. I see bad times to - day.

Chorus

Don't go a-round to-night. Well, it's

bound to take your life. There's a bad moon on the rise.

CHAPTER THREE
Bad Moon Rising

This is a great first song; It has three chords, a simple structure, and a useful strum pattern. Best of all, most people know it, and it's fun to sing along with. What's not to like? It will help to have a recorded copy of the song, to check your progress and play along with. Remember to practice twenty minutes a day, six days a week. Slow & steady does it!

QUESTIONS?

CHECK THE APPENDIX!

Step #1: This step has two parts; learn the three chords (with finger sequence), and practice the EZ strum.

Learn the chords: We need only three chords to play "Bad Moon Rising;" D, G, & A. All of these chords are fairly easy and used in many more songs, so get them down! Read the hints in the appendix if you need help and listen to the CD example so you can hear what the chord is supposed to sound like. Here are the three chords for quick reference:

D Chord	G Chord	A Chord
Finger Sequence: 1, 2, 3.	Finger Sequence: 3,2,1.	Finger Sequence: 1, 2, 3.
CD Track #13	CD Track #14	CD Track #16

Remember to arch your fingers to clear the other strings and angle your fingers toward the headstock, (look at the chord pictures). Put your fingers down one at a time!

Practice the EZ Strum: Just take the pick and strum downward on the strings. Remember to hit most of the strings and strum reasonably steady. We want this to be so simple you don't even have to look at your right hand. Just pick one of the three chords (I use G on the CD), and play it while you whang away with the EZ strum.

Track #23
EZ Strum
(G Chord)

Step #2: For Bad Moon Rising, the *easiest part** is the Chorus:

Chorus

Track #2 (A)
EZ Strum

This gives us four small tasks. (Remember the main principle, take it in small bits).

1. **PRACTICE G TO D:** Make a G chord, one finger at a time. Now visualize a D chord (remember your finger sequence for D; one, two, and three). Start that right hand strumming the EZ strum and switch! Put down one finger at a time and don't stop strumming, no matter what! Your goal is to get all three fingers down on that D without stopping the EZ strum. Once you can do that, the second goal is to get them all down in four strums or less. This step should take 15 or 20 minutes of steady practice, one day's practice session.

2. **PRACTICE D TO A:** Another day, another chord. Remember your finger sequence If you can do A with one finger, your finger order is one! Don't forget to review G to D.

3. **PRACTICE A TO G:** G reverses the finger sequence; three, two, and one.. Keep playing that EZ strum and get those fingers down in four beats. Review the two previous changes.

4. **PRACTICE D TO G:** If you play the chorus more than once, you will need to go back around to the beginning and play it again. Remember G reverses the finger sequence (3-2-1). Aim for making the switch in four beats.

Now try putting everything together and play the chorus (*slowly!*) with the EZ strum. Remember you can do anything if you take it slow enough. While you're practicing the chorus, you might as well start Step #3.

*Try to find the easiest part of a song to learn first. That way you can get used to the chords and strumming. The easy part generally has the fewest, longest held chords.

Step#3: Learn the Basic Strum Pattern:

Learn the basic strum pattern: "Bad Moon Rising" uses what I call a "medium 4" strum, it works well on any song in 4/4 time played at a medium tempo (a lot of songs!). Medium 4 is a name I use, instead of the music notation which looks like this:

Medium 4 Strum

Track #24
Medium 4 Strum
(G Chord)

You play it by strumming down on beat one and down-up on beats two, three and four. Most people add the word "and" between the last three beats to keep track of down and up strums. Practice this strum *on one chord only*, until it feels comfortable. Practice with the CD! I'm using a G chord.

Step#4: Combine the steps:

Now it's time to put the medium 4 strum you learned in step 3 with the chord progression you learned in step 2. Remember to; take each chord change separately, put down one finger at a time, and don't stop strumming. Go slow, but don't stop!

Track #2 (B)
Medium 4 Strum

Congratulations! By now you should be able to play the chorus to "Bad Moon Rising" slowly. Now use the same four part template for the verse*. Notice there are no new chord changes, you handled them all learning the chorus. It does add a challenge in the second measure, you've got to switch A to G, and G to D in two beats! Don't panic, just go extra slow with your EZ strum and keep putting those fingers down one at a time. When you get the second measure together, play the entire verse using the EZ strum before adding the medium 4 strum. Remember, learn both hands separately before putting them together!

Verse

Track #3 (A & B)
EZ Strum/Medium 4 Strum

The final challenge will be to play along with the recorded song. Now is the time to start pushing yourself! Tap your foot with the beat and strum down to match, using the EZ strum. Just play the chorus at first, and let the verse go by. Look at the chord chart to see how often & when to play each part. When you can play the chorus try the verse, then put them both together. Hard, isn't it? Remember these people are pros, so if it takes a few more weeks that's OK, you're playing Creedence!

Chapter Three Summary:

To play "Bad Moon Rising", you need; D, A, & G chords and a medium 4 strum.

After two or three weeks of light practice, (20 minutes a day, 6 days a week) you should be able to play "Bad Moon Rising" along with the track, if not with the medium 4 strum at least with the EZ strum. That mechanical feel will gradually go away as you keep reviewing and practicing. Ninety days of regular review will get it "under your fingers", and you will start to sound musical. By taking the song in small bits and learning each hand separately, you've learned a real song. Good work!

CHAPTER FOUR

Hey Joe

Originally written by Billy Roberts, this song has been performed by Jimi Hendrix, Patti Smith & Moe Bandy among others. Although it has five chords, its simple structure and common strum pattern make it a good song for beginners. Basically, it's just the same five chords over & over again. My kind of song! *(note: while the original song was written in the key of A blues*, we will play it in E blues, because it's easier!)* Try and get a recording of the song to play along with, and remember to practice twenty minutes a day, six days a week.

*The original chords are; F, C, G, D, and A.

QUESTIONS?
CHECK THE APPENDIX!

Hey Joe
Words and Music by Billy Roberts

Hey   Joe   where you going with that money in your hand?   Chasin' my woman

She run off with a - nother   man.

Verse Two and Three Lyrics

VERSE TWO: Going downtown, buy me a forty four, when I get through, that woman won't run no more.

VERSE THREE: Hey Joe, what are you gonna do? Take my pistol and kill her before I'm through.

ETC.

Copyright: ©1962. Six Palms Music Corp. dba Third Palm Music (BMI)
Used by Permission

Step #1: This step has two parts; learn five chords (with finger sequence), and practice the EZ strum.

- *Learn the chords:* We need five chords to play "Hey Joe;" C, G, D, E, and A*. All of these chords are fairly easy and they will be used in many other songs, so get them down! Read the hints in the appendix if you need help and listen to the CD example so you can hear what the chord is supposed to sound like. *The five chords are below for quick reference.*

C Chord

Finger Sequence:
1, 2, 3.

CD Track #15

G Chord

Finger Sequence:
3, 2, 1.

CD Track #14

D Chord

Finger Sequence:
1, 2, 3.

CD Track #13

E Chord

Finger Sequence:
1, 2, 3.

CD Track #17

A Chord

Finger Sequence:
1, 2, 3.

CD Track #16

Remember to arch your fingers toward the headstock and put them down one at a time!

- *Practice the EZ strum:* Take the pick and strum downward on the strings. Just hit most of the strings and strum reasonably steady. Don't even *look* at your right hand! Pick one of the five chords (I use G on the CD), and play it while you go crazy with the EZ strum.

Track #23
EZ Strum
(G Chord)

Hey Joe-Chord Chart

C G   D A E

*If you've already learned "Bad Moon Rising," you only need to learn C and E!

Step#2: Learn the easiest part using the EZ strum:

For "Hey Joe" there is only one part! That's why you should take your time on this step. We have five small tasks;

1. **PRACTICE C TO G:** G reverses the finger sequence; three, two, & one. Make a C chord, start that right hand strumming and switch! Your goal is to get all three fingers down, one at a time, within four beats. Don't stop strumming!

2. **PRACTICE G TO D:** The finger sequence for D is one, two, & three. Keep strumming!

3. **PRACTICE D TO A:** Remember your finger sequence. If you can do A with one finger, your finger order is one! Use the EZ strum and get it down in four beats.

4. **PRACTICE A TO E:** The finger sequence for E is one, two,& three. Keep wailing away with that EZ strum!

5. **PRACTICE E TO C:** Remember this is the *whole song,* so you have to go back to C to start over. The finger sequence for C is one, two, & three. Aim for making the switch in four beats.

Track #4 (A)
EZ Strum

Now try playing all five chords together *(slowly!)* with the EZ strum. Notice we're still making the changes every four beats, while during most of the song, we only have two beats per change. We're just following the main principle, and taking it in small bits. Once you can make the changes in four beats, then try three beats per change, until you can finally do it in two. (And you have *eight beats* for E, it's like a vacation!) Remember to go back around to the beginning. This is the whole song so by the time you sing all the lyrics, you'll need to play it a dozen times.

Step#3: Learn the Basic Strum Pattern:

"Hey Joe" uses what I call a "slow 4 strum", This is a useful strum pattern that works well on any song in 4/4 time that's played at a slow tempo. Slow 4 is just a name I use, instead of writing music notation. It looks like this:

Slow 4 Strum

Track #25
Slow 4 Strum
(G Chord)

Strum down, down-up on *each beat.* If you remember the goofy tune "1&a 2&a 3 little indians", and match each down, down-up strum to that, you'll have it.

Step#4: Combine the steps:

Finally it's time to put the chord progression you learned in step #2 with the Slow 4 strum you learned in step #3. Use the three parts; take each chord change separately, put down one finger at a time, and don't stop strumming! The goal is to play the entire five chord progression *slowly*, at least two times in a row non-stop.

Track #4 (B)
Slow 4 Strum

Now is the time to start pushing yourself to play with the recorded song. Take it in stages; start by tapping your foot with the beat and using the EZ strum. When you get that down, add in the slow 4 strum. Of *course* it's hard, you're playing with a pro!

Chapter Four Summary:

To play "Hey Joe", in the key of E, you need; C, G, D, A, & E chords and a slow 4 strum.

After a few weeks of light practice, you should be able to play "Hey Joe" along with the CD, at least with the EZ strum. The occasional mistake and that robotic feel will gradually go away as you continue practicing. It takes several months of regular review and practice to really get a song down and feel comfortable with it.

CHAPTER FIVE

Greensleeves (What Child Is This?)

QUESTIONS?

CHECK THE
APPENDIX!

"Greensleeves" was supposedly written by King Henry the VIII in the middle ages, a true golden oldie! The same melody is used in the Christmas song "What Child is this," so most people are familiar with this beautiful song. Locating a recording of this is difficult but not impossible, (look for it in Christmas song collections under its "Christmas name"). Remember, practice twenty minutes a day, six days a week! *(You can find the music on the next page.)*

Step #1: This step has two parts; learn five chords (with finger sequence), and practice the EZ strum.

- *Learn the chords:* You need five chords to play "Greensleeves;" Am, C, G, Em, and E. All of these chords are pretty easy, and if you learned the previous two songs you already know most of them! Remember to arch your fingers and keep putting them down one at a time in the correct order. Check the appendix and look at the pictures if you need help. *(A quick reference to the five chords you will need is located in step #2.)*

- *Practice the EZ strum:* Take the pick and strum downwards on the strings. Try to hit most of the strings and strum reasonably steady. Don't even *look* at your right hand! Pick one of the five chords (G is good, I play that on the CD) and go crazy with that strum!

Track #23
EZ Strum
(G Chord)

Greensleeves

Traditional

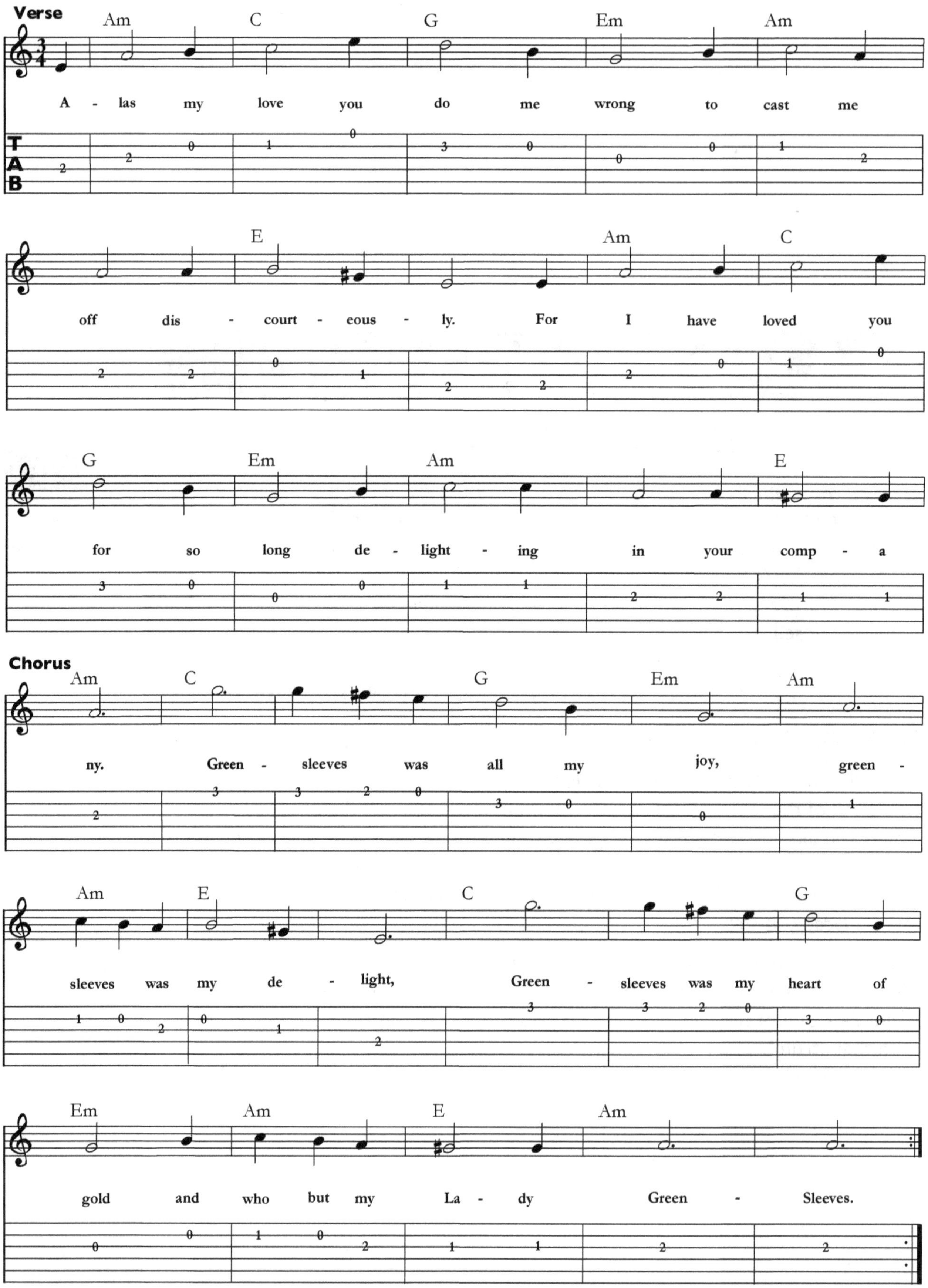

Step#2: Learn the easiest part using the EZ strum:

"Greensleeves" has two parts that are almost identical, the verse starts with an Am, and the refrain/chorus starts with a C. For that reason, I give a slight edge to the verse, I think Am is a little easier than C. We have five small tasks:

Track #5 (A)
EZ Strum

1. **PRACTICE Am TO C:** This is easy! The finger sequence for both chords is one, two, three, *and* you only have to move the third finger.

2. **PRACTICE C TO G:** G reverses the finger sequence; three, two, and one. Carefully make your C, play that EZ strum and get those fingers down to G in three beats!

3. **PRACTICE G TO Em:** The finger sequence for Em is two and three. Keep strumming *non-stop*.

4. **PRACTICE Em TO Am:** These chords are almost the same. Try to keep your fingers in formation as you switch, and just add the first finger. If that's too hard, just use the one, two, three finger sequence. Either way, don't stop strumming!

5. **PRACTICE Am TO E and E TO Am:** I've lumped both these changes together because these chords have the exact same shape and fingering. Try to keep them in formation as you switch, the one, two, three finger sequence is not necessary on this one!

Now put it all together and play the five chord changes with the EZ strum, nonstop. Go slow. "Greensleeves" is a slow song anyway, you don't have a plane to catch! Take your time and get this down before you go on.

Verse-Chord Chart

Amin	C	G	Emin	Amin		E	

Amin	C	G	Emin	Amin		E		Amin **Etc.**

Am Chord

A minor

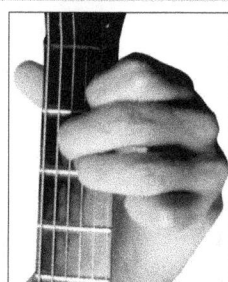

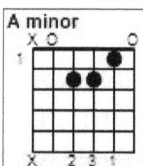

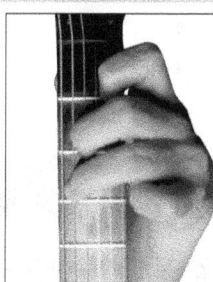

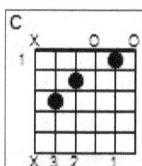

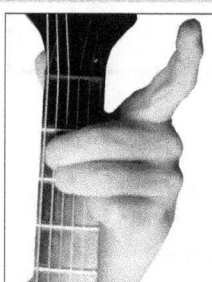

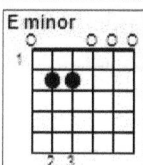

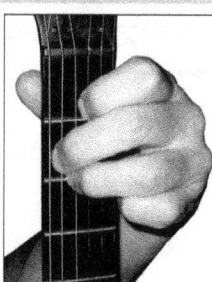

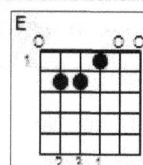

Finger Sequence: 1, 2, 3.

CD Track #19

C Chord

C

Finger Sequence: 1, 2, 3.

CD Track #15

G Chord

G

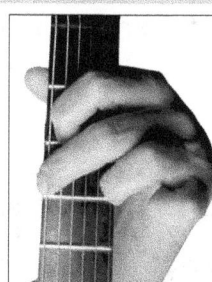

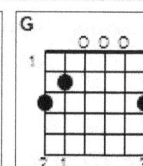

Finger Sequence: 3,2,1.

CD Track #14

Em Chord

E minor

Finger Sequence: 2,3.

CD Track #18

E Chord

E

Finger Sequence: 1, 2, 3.

CD Track #17

Step#3: Learn the Basic Strum Pattern:

"Greensleeves" is played in a ¾ or waltz strum, because it's in a ¾ time signature (see appendix). You will use it in slower, more traditional tunes like waltzes, folk and country ballads.

3/4 Strum

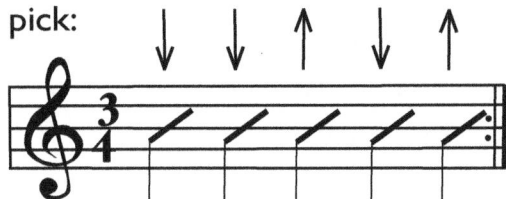

Track #27
3/4 Strum
(G Chord)

Pick a chord and practice this strum. (I'm playing G in the example.)

Step#4: Combine the steps:

Assuming that you have steps 2 and 3 down, it's time to put both hands together and play the verse with the ¾ strum. Remember; take each chord change separately, put down one finger at a time, and don't stop strumming! Once you have the changes separately, put them all together and play them slowly. Luckily, "Greensleeves" is a slow song so you won't have to go much faster. It's easy!

Track #5 (B)
3/4 Strum

The only thing left is to learn the refrain, and the only thing new about *that* is that it starts both lines with a C instead of an Am. You have one more step;

> **PRACTICE E TO C:** The finger sequence for C is one, two, three. The shape is not that different from E, so you shouldn't have too much trouble. Keep strumming.

Now play the entire refrain using the EZ strum before substituting the ¾ strum. Learn each hand separately before putting them together!

Chapter Five Summary:

To play "Greensleeves," you need a 3/4 strum and five chords; Am, C, G, Em, and E. After learning a few songs, using the Learning Template should be getting easier. "Greensleeves" used only two new chords and only a slightly different strum from the first song. You really can learn anything, if you take it in small bits and go slow!

CHAPTER SIX

The Circle Pattern (I, vi, IV, V)

QUESTIONS?

CHECK THE
APPENDIX!

Four Chords Equals Hundreds of Songs!

Although there are several circle patterns, (which just refer to a smooth progression of chords), this pattern is one of the most used in popular music: from oldies like "Last Kiss" to "Every Breath You Take," this pattern never goes out of style! For this particular song, (similar to Last Kiss) we will start on a G chord. Later on, I will introduce you to a *capo;* this handy and inexpensive device will allow you to play in different keys all over the neck. Then we can start the circle pattern on a different fret, (similar to "Every Breath You Take", played on fret two). If you don't understand what a **key** refers to, or what those funny roman numbers; I,vi,IV,V stand for (and you care), see the appendix. I will list a bunch more popular songs that follow this pattern at the end of the chapter. Locate a recording of one of the songs if you need to. (Most people can recognize this the first time they play it, so you really don't need to.) Be sure to practice regularly!

> **Step #1: This step has two parts; learn four chords (with finger sequence), and practice the EZ strum.**

- *Learn the chords:* You need four chords for this progression; G, Em, C and D. These chords are all relatively easy, so just look at the picture and check the appendix if necessary to make sure you have the correct hand position. Remember to arch your fingers and angle them back toward the headstock! *(A quick reference to the four chords you will need is located in step #2.)*

- *Practice the EZ strum:* Take the pick and strum downwards on the strings. Try to hit most of the strings and strum reasonably steady. Don't even *look* at your right hand! Pick one of the four chords (G is good, I'm playing it on the example) and strum away.

Track #23
EZ Strum
(G Chord)

Step#2: Learn the easiest part using the EZ strum:

Again, this is a one part progression so take your time. We have four small tasks;

1. **Practice G to Em:** The finger sequence for Em is two and three. Carefully arrange your fingers on the G chord, start strumming and switch one finger at a time. Don't stop! .Your goal for all of these chords is to switch in four beats.

2. **Practice Em to C:** Arch your fingers and angle them back towards the headstock to get a clear C. (finger sequence one, two, three.)

3. **Practice C to D:** The finger sequence for D is one, two, three. Keep strumming!

4. **Practice D to G:** G reverses the finger sequence (three, two, and one.) Start strumming on the D and switch one finger at a time without stopping.

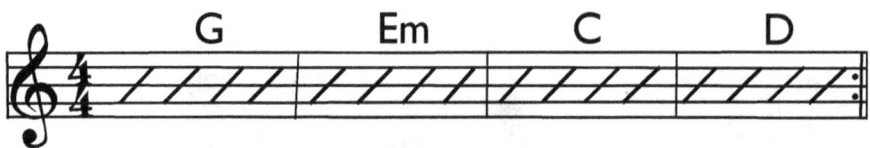

Track #6 (A)
EZ Strum

Now try playing all four chords together *slowly* and *nonstop*. You have four beats per chord change so that should make it do-able. Believe it or not, this simple progression is the main part of all the songs listed at the end of this chapter (and thousands more!). All you have to do is change the key using the capo which I'll tell you about in step #4.

G Chord

Finger Sequence:
3,2,1.

CD Track #14

Em Chord

Finger Sequence:
2, 3.

CD Track #18

C Chord

Finger Sequence:
1, 2, 3.

CD Track #15

D Chord

Finger Sequence:
1, 2, 3.

CD Track #13

Step#3: Learn the Basic Strum Pattern:

Although you can play this pattern using all of the strums in this report, I'm going to introduce a strum pattern I call the *oldies strum*. You can call it whatever you want. It looks like this in music notation:

Oldies Strum

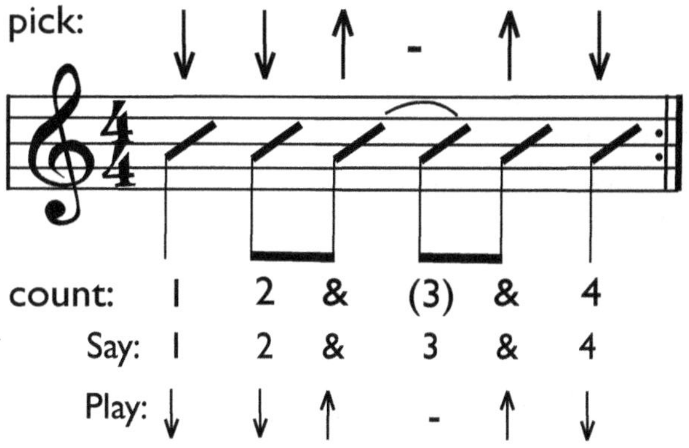

Track #28
Oldies Strum
(G Chord)

It's easier to play this strum than to read it. (I used to call it the parochial school strum because it's generally the first strum you learn at church camp!) Listen to the CD example and strum along. I'm playing a G.

Step#4: Combine the steps:

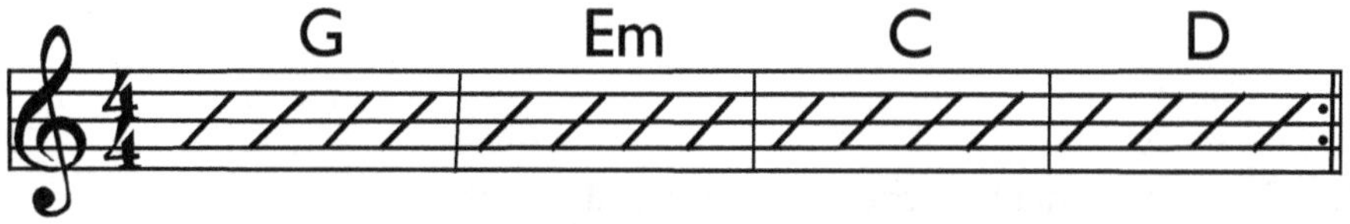

Track #6 (B)
Oldies Strum

Now it's time to combine the circle progression you learned in step #2 with the strum pattern in step #3. Take each chord change separately, put down one finger at a time and don't stop strumming! Play the entire progression *slowly*, nonstop. This should remind you of a million songs. In fact, it probably is a million songs! For that to happen, however, you'll need to play it in different keys (see appendix), and the easiest way to do *that* is with a capo.

A **capo** is most often a bar that clamps over the fretboard and is held in place with elastic or a lever. Notice in the picture that I have it as close behind the fret as possible. A capo allows you to raise the pitch, (and change the key) of your guitar. The higher the capo, the higher the pitch. This allows you to play the song in many keys, up to six more *without changing the chord forms.* You can go higher, but past the sixth fret, things sound a little dinky in my opinion. Look at Column I in the chart below.

Track #7
Oldies Strum
(capo fret 2)

What starts as G Em C and D turns into an A F#m D and E when you put the capo on the second fret. Just pretend the capo is fret zero and play the same four chords, it's automatic! The capo becomes the new zero fret. Listen to the example. These are the chords used in Every Breath You Take, (although I would use a simple rock/blues strum instead).

Column I

Fret	I	vi	IV	V
0	G	Em	C	D
1	Ab	Fm	Db	Eb
2	A	F#m	D	E
3	Bb	Gm	Eb	F
4	B	G#m	E	F#
5*	C	Am	F	G
6*	Db	Bbm	Gb	Ab

Column II

Fret	I	vi	IV	V
0*	C	Am	F	G
1*	Db	Bbm	Gb	Ab
2	D	Bm	G	A
3	Eb	Cm	Ab	Bb
4	E	C#m	A	B
5	F	Dm	Bb	C
6	Gb	Ebm	Cb	Db

* Notice that frets 5 and 6 on column I are the same as frets O and I on column II, you can play either way!)

As a final note, if you look at the Column II chart to the right, you will see the same circle pattern starting on a C cord. This requires two new chords; A minor (Am), and the dreaded F. A minor is easy, almost like a C, just move the third finger. This leaves the dreaded F chord. The main secret to a decent F is to roll your entire left hand toward the headstock as you make the chord. Look at the picture to make sure you have the correct hand position, put your fingers down one at a time and arch the second and third fingers! While you're getting the circle pattern down with the EZ strum, I might as well introduce the 6/8 strum.

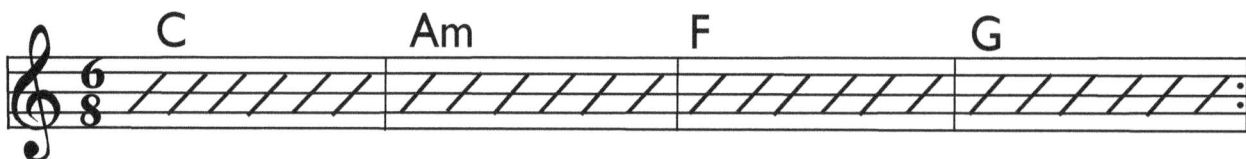

Am Chord

A minor

Finger Sequence:
1, 2, 3.

CD Track #19

F Chord

F

Finger Sequence:
1, 2, 3.

CD Track #20

6/8 Strum

pick: ↓ ↓ ↑ ↓ ↑ ↓ ↓ ↑ ↓ ↑

Track #26
6/8 Strum

count: ① 2 & 3 & ④ 5 & 6 &

Say: ① 2 & 3 & ④ 5 & 6 &

Play: ↓ ↓ ↑ ↓ ↑ ↓ ↓ ↑ ↓ ↑

The 6/8 strum is also used in a circle pattern, as well as many popular songs like "House of the Rising Sun". It's used when the song has a **time signature** of 6/8. (If you don't know what that means, check the appendix.)

Track #8
Key of C
EZ/6/8 Strum

That's quite a mouthful isn't it? Since you can't really play this strum at a decent speed while saying all those numbers (unless you're a professional auctioneer), most people just count the first and fourth beats. Notice how close the two circle patterns sound and the fact that you can play another six keys using the capo. That's all twelve of them, you can now play this pattern in any key. You are cool!

Chapter Six Summary:

By using a capo and a half-dozen chords you can play a circle pattern in any key, and by plugging in any one of our standard strums it's possible to play thousands of songs. The four chords in this pattern; I, vi, IV, and V are so popular you can re-arrange them in different sequences into even more songs! Following this summary I've included a partial list of songs that follow a circle pattern as well as a few that use different arrangements of the same four chords. Just put the capo on the correct fret to produce the chords you need for that song, plug in an appropriate strum and go! Easy!

Songs using the Circle Pattern:

(Just find the first chord in columns I or II, the rest of the chords will be there!)

- Every Breath You Take (Police) Key A
- All I Have To Do Is Dream (Everly Bros.) Key C
- Blue Moon (Elvis) Key G
- Breaking Up Is Hard To Do (Neil Sedaka) Key B
- Duke Of Earl (Shandler) Key E
- Earth Angel (Penguins) Key C
- Baby (Justin Beiber) Key Eb

- Heart And Soul (Cleftones) Key C
- Runaround Sue (Dion) Key C
- Teenager In Love (Dion) Key C
- Why Do Fools Fall In Love? (Frankie Lymon) Key C
- You Send Me (Sam Cooke) Key G
- Last Kiss (Cavaliers/Pearl Jam) Keys E/G

Songs Using the I, vi, IV, V chords in a Different Sequence:

(Just find the first chord in columns I or II, the rest of the chords will be there!)

- I'm Going Home (Daughtry) Key G
- Good (Better Than Ezra) Key G
- Time Of Your Life (Green Day) Key G
- Boulevard Of Broken Dreams (Green Day) Key Ab
- Viva La Vida (Coldplay) Key G

- glycerine (bush) key F
- mine (taylor swift) key G
- 15 (taylor swift) key G
- every rose has its' thorn (poison) key G
- don't stop believin' (journey) key E

CHAPTER SEVEN

Scarborough Fair

QUESTIONS?

CHECK THE
APPENDIX!

This is a classic English ballad recorded by Simon and Garfunkel, Sarah Brightman, Glen Campbell, and Justin Hayward (Moody Blues), among others. This song has four easy chords and a fairly simple repeating structure. It uses a ¾ strum, (also called a waltz strum), used in many slower tempo songs. Locate a recording if you need to, but you probably know this one! *(You can find the music on the next page.)*

Step #1: This step has two parts; learn four chords (with finger sequence), and practice the EZ strum.

- Learn the chords: You need four chords to play "Scarborough Fair;" Am, C, G, and D. All of these chords are fairly easy for most people, with the C chord being the biggest hassle. The main "secret" to a decent C is to roll your entire left hand toward the headstock as you make the chord. Check the chord picture to make sure you have the correct hand position. As always, remember to arch your fingers and put them down one at a time when you make the chords!

- Practice the EZ strum: Take the pick and strum downwards on the strings. Try to hit most of the strings and strum reasonably steady. Don't even *look* at your right hand! Pick one of the four chords and play it while you blonk away with the EZ strum. (I'm playing G in the example)

Track #23
EZ Strum
(G Chord)

Scarborough Fair

Traditional English Ballad

Verse Two Lyrics

VERSE TWO: Tell her to make me a cambric shirt. Parsley, sage, rosemary, and thyme. Without no seams nor needle work. Then she'll be a true love of mine.

ETC...

Step#2: Learn the easiest part using the EZ strum:

Like "Hey Joe" this song only has one part, so take your time on this step. We have seven small tasks;

Track #9 (A)
EZ Strum

1. **PRACTICE Am TO G:** The finger sequence for G is three, two, and one. Make the Am chord, start that EZ strum and get those fingers down in three beats!

2. **PRACTICE G TO Am:** The sequence for Am is one, two, and three. The goal is to strum non-stop, and switch the chord in three beats.

3. **PRACTICE Am TO C:** This is easy! You only have to move the third finger.

4. **PRACTICE C TO Am:** See step three.

5. **PRACTICE Am TO D:** The finger sequence for D is one, two, three. Keep strumming.

6. **PRACTICE D TO Am:** Step five in reverse. The sequence is still one, two, three.

7. **PRACTICE C TO G:** The finger sequence for G is three, two, and one. This is almost the same as step one. Aim for making the switch in three beats or less.

While these are the only chord changes needed in "Scarborough Fair," you will have to play some changes more than once as you play the entire song. Your goal for this step is to play the song all the way through using the EZ strum. Take your time, it's a slow song anyway!

Am Chord

A minor

Finger Sequence:
1, 2, 3.

CD Track #19

C Chord

C

Finger Sequence:
1, 2, 3.

CD Track #15

G Chord

G

Finger Sequence:
3, 2, 1.

CD Track #14

D Chord

D

Finger Sequence:
1, 2, 3.

CD Track #13

Step#3: Learn the Basic Strum Pattern:

"Scarborough Fair" is played in a ¾ or waltz strum, because it's in a ¾ **time signature** (see appendix). It's used in slower, more traditional tunes like waltzes, folk and country ballads. Pick a chord and practice this strum (I'm playing G in the example).

3/4 Strum

pick: ↓ ↓ ↑ ↓ ↑

Track #27
3/4 Strum
(G Chord)

count: 1　2　&　3　&
Say: 1　2　&　3　&
Play: ↓　↓　↑　↓　↑

Step#4: Combine the steps:

Now it's time to put the chord progression you learned in step two with the ¾ strum you learned in step three. Remember, take each chord change separately, put down one finger at a time, and don't stop strumming! Your goal is to play the entire progression *slowly,* non-stop. If you have a recorded version of the song, start by tapping your foot to the beat and playing along with the EZ strum. When you can do that, try adding the ¾ strum. If you don't have a copy, just try playing fast enough so the lyrics can sung at a decent speed. Congratulations, you are now qualified to play at Renaissance festivals anywhere!

Track #9 (B)
3/4 Strum

Chapter Seven Summary:

To play "Scarborough Fair" you need; Am, C, G, and D chords and a ¾ strum.

Practicing twenty minutes a day, six days a week is all you need to get this (or any easy) song down. It may not sound very musical at first, but regular review will get it "under your fingers," and you'll become confident when you play it.

CHAPTER EIGHT

12 Bar Blues (I, IV, V Progression)

QUESTIONS?

CHECK THE APPENDIX!

Three Chords Equals Hundreds More Songs!

What do Johnny B. Goode, The Batman TV Theme, and Tush by Z.Z. Top, all have in common? They are all based on a 12 bar blues song form! Over the years, right up to the present hundreds of hit songs have followed this instantly recognizable chord progression. Best of all, it's easy! Just three chords and twelve measures (bars) of music is all that stands between you and literally hundreds of rock and blues songs. Notice the Roman numbers, I IV V; this means we can play this chord progression in any key, like the Circle Pattern in chapter 6. That's how you can play lots of songs! Definitely get this one down. I will give a much bigger list of songs that follow this pattern at the end of this chapter.

> **Step #1: This step has two parts; learn three chords (with finger sequence), and practice the EZ strum.**

- *Learn the chords:* Although the 12 bar blues pattern uses three chords we will only have to learn *two* forms, called by most, **power chords.** Power chords are the easiest form of *moveable chords,* meaning they keep the same shape as they move up the neck. Since the name of the chord changes each time you change frets, you can play a dozen chords with one shape!* The power chord's "official" name is a Perfect 5th interval, but everybody calls it a power chord instead because it's easier. It's written with a 5; E5, G5, etc., means they want a power chord. There are two types of power chords called amazingly enough, type 1 and type 2. Ready?

*See table on page 53 for a complete list of all chord names and locations.

TYPE 1: A type 1 chord is named from the note your first finger plays on the sixth string, eg. fifth fret is A, eighth fret is C, etc. Let's try an A on the fifth fret:

- put the first finger on the sixth string, fifth fret.
- put the third finger on the fifth string, seventh fret. Put down one finger at a time *(Hint: mute out the fourth string by curving your third finger a little, this will help muffle any bad notes you might accidentally hit.)*

Type 1 Power Chord

Finger Sequence:
1,3.

CD Track #21

TYPE 2: A type 2 chord is named from the note your first finger plays on the fifth string, eg. fifth fret is D, eighth fret is F, etc. Let's try a D on the fifth fret:

- put the first finger down on the fifth string, fifth fret.
- put the third finger down on the fourth string, seventh fret. Remember, put down one finger at a time! *(hint; mute out the sixth string by touching it with your first finger a little, this will muffle it in case you accidentally hit it while strumming.)*

Type 2 Power Chord

Finger Sequence:
1,3.

CD Track #22

- *Practice the EZ strum:* With power chords it's a little different. You still take the pick and strum downward, you just have to aim a little better. Instead of hitting most of the strings, strum only the sixth, fifth, and fourth strings. *Don't* hit the first, second and third! You only want to hear the strings you press when you strum a power chord. If you mute out the strings I told you about in the hints you should be OK, (The CD example illustrates the EZ Rock/Blues Strum, explained in step three.)

Track #29
EZ Rock/Blues Strum
(Type I Power Chord, A)

This ends the first lesson. It's only included two easy chord forms and a slightly modified strum. Be sure to look and listen to the examples, get those power chords *down* before you go any further!

Step#2: Learn the easiest part using the EZ strum:

A (I)*

count 1& 2& 3& 4& etc.

D (IV)　　　　　　　　　　　A (I)

E (V)　　　　　　　　　　　A (I)

Track #10 (A)
EZ Rock/Blues Strum

*The Roman numbers beside the chord name refer to its place in the key. This is explained in step four and the appendendix.

A 12 bar blues pattern gets its name from its length, it's twelve bars (measures) long! You just keep repeating the pattern to play the song. As I mentioned in the first lesson, although there are three chords in this pattern, we only play two forms; type 1 and type 2 power chords. There are four small tasks;

1. **Practice A (type 1) to D (type 2):** Switch one finger at a time. The finger sequence for power chords is always one and three. All you are doing is moving the power chord over one string, from type 1 to type 2, you're still on fret five. Remember to mute the unwanted strings. If you do this correctly you won't have to look at your strumming hand, it doesn't matter!

2. **Practice D (type 2) to A (type 1):** This is just step one backwards. Now you are moving the power chord back to the sixth string using the same one and three finger sequence. Use the EZ strum and don't stop!

3. **Practice A (type 1) to E (type 2):** This is the most challenging part. You have to switch from a type 1 to a type 2 and you have to jump two frets, from fret five to fret seven This isn't so bad if you notice that the top note of your type 1 A chord is the same as the root of your type 2 E chord. Just trade fingers! Take it slow and keep strumming.

4. **Practice E (type 2) to A (type 1):** This is step three backwards, so reverse the procedure. Since a 12 bar blues song, like Johnny B. Goode, etc., consists of playing the same pattern over and over again (really!) you will need to start the pattern over.

Your goal for the week is to play the entire 12 bar pattern non-stop using the EZ strum. Do it slow, but *do it!*

Step#3: Learn the Rock/blues strum:

There are two versions of this strum, the easiest is simply a faster version of the EZ strum. In musical terms, instead of playing quarter notes (EZ strum), you play eighth notes.

EZ Rock/Blues Strum

*Try to hit only the 4th, 5th, and 6th strings.

Track #29
EZ Rock/Blues Strum
(Type 1 Power Chord, A)

Notice the extra word "and" between the numbers. If you say " one and two and three and four and" and strum on each word, you'll get the strum. Listen to the example! Notice you are playing twice as fast even though the beat is the same. That's because you are putting 2 notes in every beat, split 50/50. SO WHERE'S THE BLUES? I'm glad you asked. You can get a blues feel by giving the notes a slightly different accent. Play the first note of each pair a little longer (2/3 of the beat) than the second note (1/3 of the beat). (EX.) Since this blues variation has to do with 3's you will often see a 3 above the 1/8 notes. Be sure and practice along with the CD to get the feel. That's it!

You can get a cool variation of this strum by adding your little finger (fourth finger). If you normally only rotate your little finger in your ear, or poke it out when you drink tea, it will surprise you to know you can also play guitar with it! Since this advanced strum does involve stretching your little finger, consider it optional.

Advanced Rock/Blues Strum

* Add little finger on beats 2 and 4 only.

Track #30
Advanced Rock/Blues Strum
(Type 1 Power Chord, A)

Do the EZ Rock/Blues strum as before, but add your little finger two frets above your third finger on the power chord (same string), on beats two & four only. Listen to the example, look at the diagram and play along with it until you get the idea. (I'm playing a type 1 A on the fifth fret.)

- add the little finger on the second and fourth beats *only* (not the ands).
- If you play slow with a triplet (three) feel, you have a blues strum. Faster with a straight eighths feel gives you a rock strum.

HINT: If you can't make the little finger stretch, just start higher up the neck, like fret ten. The frets are closer together up there, so you won't have to stretch as far. When you can play on fret ten, move down to nine, etc. until you can play it on fret five. (Try playing it on fret one, ouchy!)

Remember the advanced strum is optional, if you have too much trouble stick with the EZ Rock/Blues strum for now. The important thing is to get the 12 bar pattern down.

Step#4: This lesson has two parts; Play the 12 bar blues with either of the rock/blues strums, and learning to change keys by moving the I IV V pattern.

Remember the advanced strum is optional, if you have too much trouble stick with the EZ Rock/Blues strum for now. The important thing is to get the 12 bar pattern down.

Track #11
Advanced Rock
Strum / Blues Strum

- *Play a 12 bar blues pattern using the EZ rock/blues strum, (or the advanced strum if you're feeling lucky)*; Basically, this isn't much harder than lesson #2, you just strum a little faster. It's easier using the blues version of the strum, since you play it slower. Remember; take each change separately, switch one finger at a time, and don't stop strumming! After you get the blues version down, start working on the rock variation. It's faster, and may take awhile. Listen to the example.

- *Changing keys;* You may have noticed the Roman numerals listed with the chords in the 12 bar music example presented in lesson #2. That's because the the three power chords used form a **I IV V pattern (see Theory section in appendix)**. If you look at the *diagrams below,* you can see what I mean:
  - Diagram A shows the three chord roots for the 12 bar blues; A, D,&E..
  - Diagram B changes the chord names; (A,D,E) to Roman numerals (I IV V*). Notice how the three chords form an upside-down "L" shape.
  - Diagram C shows how you can move this shape up and down the neck, plug in the power chords, and play in any key! (the I chord is always the name of the key). In this example, I've moved the I IV V pattern to fret three, now I IV V has become G C D (diagram D). Look at the examples and check the power chord chart. Changing keys is easy with moveable chords, you don't even need a capo!

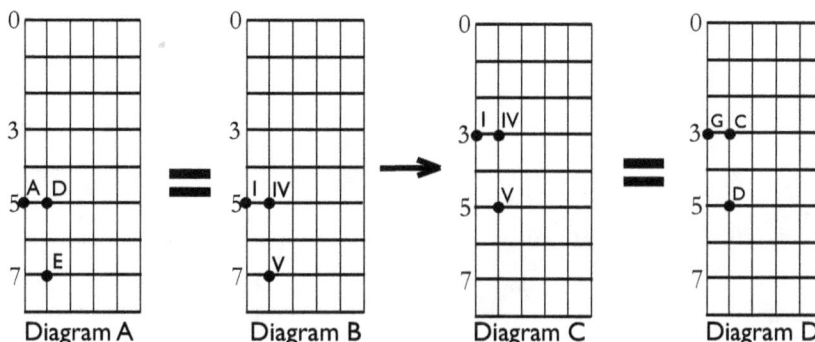

Diagram A = Diagram B → Diagram C = Diagram D

Chapter Eight Summary:

To play a 12 Bar Blues Pattern, you need; two types of moveable chords and a rock/blues strum.

You can play literally thousands of songs with the 12 bar pattern. The songs I've listed here are just a fraction. You can even change keys by moving this pattern up and down the neck! (see example, just move the same three chord pattern to another fret and play those three chords in the same 12 bar sequence) Congratulations, with this 12 bar pattern and all the potential songs you can play with it, you're ready to start the_____(lounge act, garage band, cheesy wedding outfit, etc.) of your dreams!

12 Bar Blues Pattern Songs:

- Johnny B. Goode (Chuck Berry) Key A
- Roll Over Beethoven (Chuck Berry) Key E
- Pride And Joy (S. R. Vaughn) Key E
- The Sky Is Cryin' (King/ S.R. Vaughn) Key C
- Statesboro Blues (McTell /Allman Bros.) Key D
- One Way Out (Williamson/Allman Bros.) Key A
- Crossroads (Johnson/Cream) Key A
- Dizzy Miss Lizzy (Little Richard) Key A
- What'd I Say (Ray Charles) Key E
- Batman (TV) Key G
- Tush (ZZ Top) Key G
- Steamroller Blues (James Taylor) Key E

*Like the Circle Progression, the I, IV, V Pattern forms the basis for thousands more songs. From oldies like "Louie Louie" and "Wild Thing" to punk rock ("Blitzkrieg Bop" by the Ramones), to country hits like "Family Tradition" by Hank Williams Jr. Just find the first chord in the pattern, the rest will be there!

CHAPTER NINE

Summary

QUESTIONS?

CHECK THE APPENDIX!

Throughout this report I've emphasized *go slow and take it in small bits!* You've learned how to split the big job of learning a song into a four-step process that allows you to learn each hand separately before putting them together. We then covered six different songs and progressions that showed this process in action, (you also learned ten chord forms and six strums!). Now that you are a guitar player, the next goal is transferring this knowledge into learning the kind of music *you* want to play. There are several ways to do this:

- Get a friend who plays to show you. (lucky you!)

- Figure it out yourself. (skillful you!)

- Purchase the sheet music, or try the web.

If you could swing the first two, you wouldn't be reading this, so I'm going to explore the third choice; various forms of written music you will encounter.

While there are several ways to write music for rhythm guitar, they all boil down to some kind of *chord chart.* Again, we're talking fairly simple popular music, not classical, jazz or speed metal. A chord chart only tells you two things for sure;

1. **What chords to play:** Some charts will show you chord diagrams and some will only tell you the name. With twelve or so chord forms, you can fake your way through most songs, but it's a good idea to get a chord book in case you need it.

2. **How long to play them:** Usually the directions are vague (moderate rock), to non-existent (you don't even get the number of beats). You need to know a variety of strum patterns so you can listen to a song, select the best pattern to use and start playing.

I will give a few examples of the different ways you might encounter a chord chart:

1. **Sheet Music:**

Notice out of all this information, all you get is the guitar chord name and the length of time you're supposed to play it. In this case, the time signature says 4/4 so four beats in a measure. (See appendix.) You don't get any directions on how to strum it, except for "moderate rock", whatever that means.
This is why I'm not too interested in teaching you to read music (with one exception, as we'll see).

2. **Fake Book:**

This example still only gives the chord name and length of time to play it. You still have no strum pattern and only sketchy tempo information.

3. **Lyric Sheet/Chords:**

You find this a lot in church and summer camps. For this to work, *somebody* has to know the song, since all you have is a string of words with chords on top. If *nobody* knows the song the results can be hilarious.

4. **Tablature:**

4. (con't) Finally we get exactly what we need! Tablature (tab for short) gives an overhead view of the fingerboard. Each of the 6 lines represents a string and the numbers written on the lines tell what frets to play. You read the tab chart from left to right, not top to bottom. Notes stacked on top of each other means that you play them together, like a chord. You will find tablature in commercial song books and on the web. Both ways have good points and bad points:

- **Song Books:** The most complete and accurate, also include *rhythm notation* which helps with actually playing the song, if you can understand it. (see appendix) Costs money and not available for *everything*.
- **The Web:** Free! Lots of choices. Quality ranges from very good to very bad. Definitely better than nothing. Just type in the song name + guitar tabs on your search engine.

Whatever way you obtain your music, don't try to play difficult songs yet. You can tell songs will be difficult if they contain a lot of chords, or you see a lot of #s and bs, (which means bar chords). Aim for songs with four to six chords and few, if any, #/bs. Obviously, lead guitar is beyond the scope of this report, as are classical and jazz. For those, you will need further instruction.

Tablature

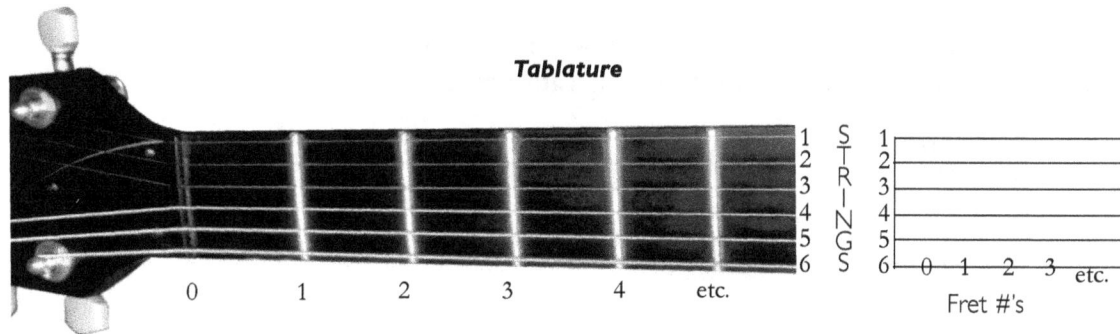

Fret #'s

Further Instruction:

You can either do it yourself, with books, DVD's, and various web-sites/videos* or look for a teacher. No matter what path you choose, try to state your goals clearly. What do you want? Help with strumming? Lead guitar? Fingerpicking? Learn more songs? The better you know your goals the easier it will be to find help. With that in mind, here are a few tips:

- **Do It Yourself:** Pick up a few guitar magazines at the news stand, check their websites. Most magazines want to keep their reputations, so you can trust (mostly) their recommendations/info. Type in "guitar tabs" on your search engine, bug the salesmen in music stores, and definitely look for other players to jam with. Good luck!

- **Find A Teacher:** Ask other guitar players who *they* recommend. If one teacher's name keeps coming up, that's a good sign. Formal education isn't necessary, but knowledge, competence and kindness are. Music stores use teachers to sell merchandise, they aren't necessarily better. When you talk to a teacher, besides asking the price, credentials, etc., state your goals and ask what they can do to help you reach them. "I just want to play good" is not a goal! Ask for a trial lesson, show them where you are as a player and state your goals. They should give you a clear idea of what you need to do and how to get there. If they don't, keep looking! Most teachers charge on a monthly basis, so don't sign up for long term contracts. Private lessons tend to be unstructured, and it's easy for both student and teacher to be lulled into a rut. Keep your goals in mind and your lessons on track!

*See Appendix for a partial list of magazines, online, and mail order stores, and tab sites.

Chapter Nine Summary:

You *can* play guitar! Just pick easy songs (at first), and go slow. Split your task into small bits, and don't try to learn two things at once!

- **Left Hand:** memorize your chords, and choose a finger sequence (put them down one at a time).

- Use the EZ strum, so you can focus on your left hand. Taking one chord change at a time, practice changing chords without stopping the strum.

- **Right Hand:** choose the best basic strum for your song and practice that with one chord, so you can focus on your right hand while you get the strum pattern down. If the music gives you the pattern in rhythm notation, and you can read it, use that instead.

- Finally combine both hands and switch chords using the correct strum.

And if all else fails, *GO SLOW!* You can do anything if you take it in small enough bits and go slow enough.

Congratulations! I hope this report has helped you on your way. Playing guitar can be a lot of fun and rewarding, although learning it can be frustrating at times! Relax and enjoy the journey.

Best wishes on your musical path!

JIM BECKWITH

APPENDIX

Reference Section

This is the appendix. It's basically a collection of short answers to various questions you might have on equipment, chords, strums, etc. Since I don't know your level of knowledge, and I didn't want to clutter up the book with endless explanations and re-hashings, I just put the "nuts & bolts" here. You can refer to it if you need it. All underlined terms are explained here.

Anatomy of the Guitar:

Electric Guitar:

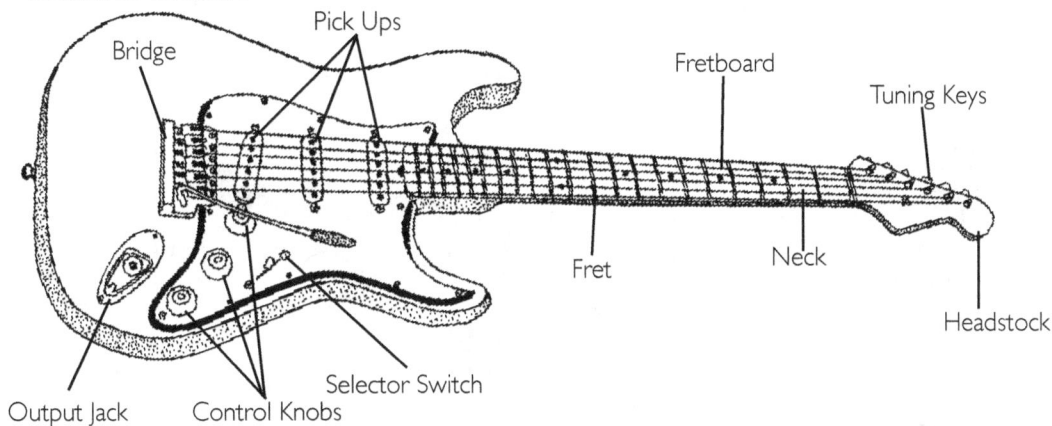

Acoustic Guitar:

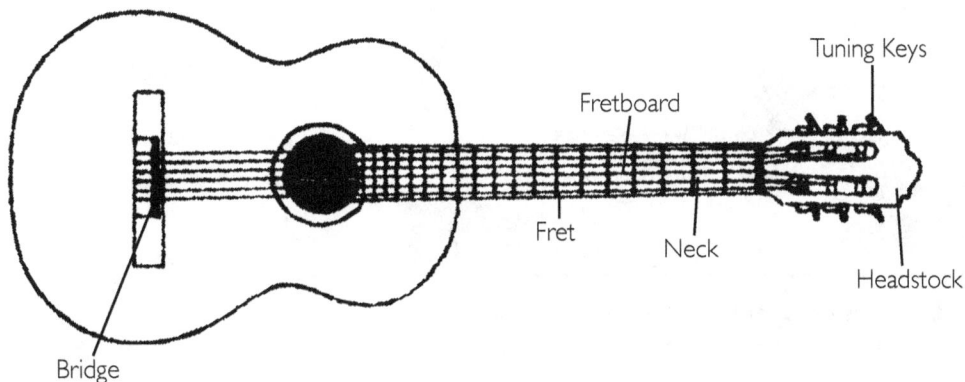

Reading a Chord Diagram:

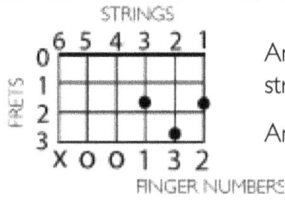

An "x" means to mute the string by allowing an adjacent finger to touch an open string and prevent it from sounding when you strum the chord.

An "o" means open string, no fingers needed!

Chords: Finger sequence: Always put your fingers down one at a time.

First Finger D → **Second Finger D** → **D Chord (Third Finger)**

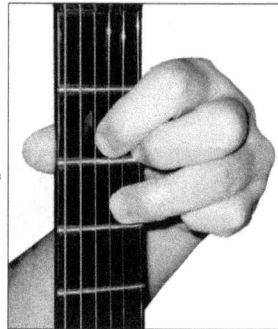

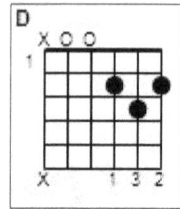

Finger Sequence: 1,2,3.

CD Track #12

D Chord
Finger Sequence: 1, 2, 3.

CD Track #13

G Chord
Finger Sequence: 3,2,1.

CD Track #14

C Chord
Finger Sequence: 1, 2, 3.

CD Track #15

A Chord
Finger Sequence: 1, 2, 3.

CD Track #16

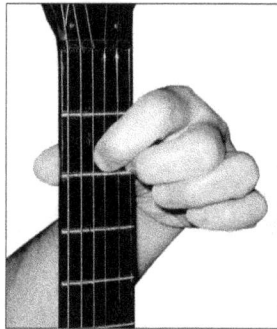

Easy A Chord
Finger Sequence: 1.

CD Track #16

E Chord
Finger Sequence: 1, 2, 3.

CD Track #17

Em Chord
Finger Sequence: 2, 3.

CD Track #18

Am Chord
Finger Sequence: 1, 2, 3.

CD Track #19

F Chord
Finger Sequence: 1, 2, 3.

CD Track #20

*Hint: Substitute plain major and minor chords for 7ths; ex. D for D7 or A minor for A minor 7. It will sound fine.

Type 1 Power Chord

Finger Sequence:
1,3.

CD Track #21

Type 2 Power Chord

Finger Sequence:
1,3.

CD Track #22

*Type 1-Major

Finger Sequence:
1,2,3,4.

*Type 1-minor

Finger Sequence:
1, 3,4.

*Type 2-Major

Finger Sequence:
1, 3.

*Type 2-minor

Finger Sequence:
1,2,3,4.

Power Chord Chart

Type 1 Power Chord

Fret	Chord
0	E
1	F
2	F#/Gb
3	G
4	G#/Ab
5	A
6	A#/Bb
7	B
8	C
9	C#/Db
10	D
11	D#/Eb
12	E

Type 2 Power Chord

Fret	Chord
0	A
1	A#/Bb
2	B
3	C
4	C#/Db
5	D
6	D#/Eb
7	E
8	F
9	F#/Gb
10	G
11	G#/Ab
12	A

*I have added full major and minor bar chord diagrams. While they are beyond the scope of this book, learning them will eventually allow you to play almost anything! Keep your first finger straight.

Sharps and Flats:

Those symbols you see on the chart above are called **sharps and flats.** Don't be afraid, they're just modifiers.

- **# Sharps:** Tell you to raise the chord one fret higher. (For example, from the third fret to the fourth fret.)
- **b Flats:** Tell you to lower the chord one fret. (For example, from the fifth fret to the fourth fret.)

The reason you see two names on fret four is because it takes its name from the notes on either side.

G# and Ab are the same note! You can call these notes either name right now, either G# or Ab. (It *will* make a difference if you take a music theory class, but right now, who cares?)

Strums:

EZ Strum CD Track #23

pick: ↓ ↓ ↓ ↓

count: 1 2 3 4
Say: 1 2 3 4
Play: ↓ ↓ ↓ ↓

Track #'s 23-30
Tracks #23-28 played on a G Chord
Tracks #29 and #30 played on a Type I
Power Chord, 5th Fret

Medium 4 Strum CD Track #24

pick: ↓ ↓↑ ↓↑ ↓↑

* ↓ = pick down
  ↑ = pick up

count: 1 2 & 3 & 4 &
Say: 1 2 & 3 & 4 &
Play: ↓ ↓↑ ↓↑ ↓↑

Slow 4 Strum CD Track #25

pick: ↓ ↓↑ ↓ ↓↑ ↓ ↓↑ ↓ ↓↑

count: 1 & a 2 & a 3 & a 4 & a
Say: 1 & a 2 & a 3 & a 4 & a
Play: ↓ ↓↑ ↓ ↓↑ ↓ ↓↑ ↓ ↓↑

6/8 Strum CD Track #26

pick: ↓ ↓ ↑ ↓ ↑ ↓ ↓ ↑ ↓ ↑

count: ① 2 & 3 & ④ 5 & 6 &
Say: ① 2 & 3 & ④ 5 & 6 &
Play: ↓ ↓ ↑ ↓ ↑ ↓ ↓ ↑ ↓ ↑

3/4 Strum   CD Track #27

pick:

count: 1   2   &   3   &
Say: 1   2   &   3   &
Play: ↓   ↓   ↑   ↓   ↑

Oldies Strum   CD Track #28

pick:

count: 1   2   &   (3)   &   4
Say: 1   2   &   (3)   &   4
Play: ↓   ↓   ↑   -   ↑   ↓

EZ Rock/Blues Strum   CD Track #29

pick:

count: 1 &   2 &   3 &   4 &
Say: 1 &   2 &   3 &   4 &
Play: ↓ ↓   ↓ ↓   ↓ ↓   ↓ ↓

Advanced Rock/Blues Strum   CD Track #30

pick:

* Add little finger on
beats 2 and 4 only.

count: 1 &   *2 &   3 &   *4 &
Say: 1 &   **2** &   3 &   **4** &
Play: ↓ ↓   *↓ ↓   ↓ ↓   *↓ ↓

Music Theory: Understanding Keys:

For our purposes, a **key** is simply a group of seven chords and a scale that go together. There are twelve keys, one for each note in the **chromatic scale** (a chromatic scale contains every possible note, and there are only twelve notes, see the chart below).

You can play any combination of chords in a key, they all sound good together. Scales are used to play **melody**; vocalists, lead guitar, horn players, keyboards etc. all use scales. Chords are used for **harmony**; rhythm guitar and keyboard players are the main instruments for harmony. Since this is a book for beginners, I'm not including a scale diagram or any instructions on lead guitar, that's another report. However, I *am* including a chart of the chords in all twelve keys below along with their **number names**. You see pros refer to chords by Roman numbers, which tell the chords' place in the key or its degree. The first chord in the key is called the I chord, the fourth chord in the key is called the IV chord, etc. Since a key consists of seven chords, you have seven Roman numbers/degrees. Why do we give chords number names? It makes it easy to change keys! If a song uses a I,IV,V chord progression in the key of C, you can play the I,IV,V chords in the same sequence in the key of G. That's how you change keys! It's just a line by line substitution. Below is a chart of all twelve keys. The Roman numbers are on the top line; upper case Roman numbers mean the chord is major, lower case means minor, lower case plus the degree sign means diminished chord. Below that the chords for all twelve keys are listed.

**Key Names	Professional Chord Names (Gray)/Actual Chords Below						
	I major	ii minor	iii minor	IV major	V major	vi minor	°vii Diminished
A	A	Bmin	C#min	D	E	F#min	G#dim
A#/Bb *	Bb	Cmin	Dmin	Eb	F	Gmin	Adim
B	B	C#min	D#min	E	F#	G#min	A#dim
C	C	Dmin	Emin	F	G	Amin	Bdim
C#/Db *	Db	Ebmin	Fmin	Gb	Ab	Bbmin	Cdim
D	D	Emin	F#min	G	A	Bmin	C#dim
D#/Eb *	Eb	Fmin	Gmin	Ab	Bb	Cmin	Ddim
E	E	F#min	G#min	A	B	C#min	D#dim
F	F	Gmin	Amin	Bb	C	Dmin	Edim
F#/Gb *	Gb	Abmin	Bbmin	Cb	Db	Ebmin	Fdim
G	G	Amin	Bmin	C	D	Emin	F#dim
G#/Ab *	Ab	Bbmin	Cmin	Db	Eb	Fmin	Gdim

*When keys have two possible names (for example, A# or Bb) I have chosen the flat key.
**The chromatic scale and the key names are the same.

Changing keys is easy! Say you're playing a song in the key of G. The chords are; G,D,Em,C. Looking in the chart you notice those chords have the Roman numbers; I,V, vi,IV in the key of G. If you want to change the song to the key of C, just locate the chords that have the same number names in the key of C (I,V,vi,IV chords in C are; C,G,Am,F) and substitute those chords. That's all there is to it!

Why would you want to change keys? To make it easier to play or sing! If the chords are too hard in one key (like Db), change the chords to an easy key (like C). If a song is too high or low to sing comfortably, switch to an easier key to sing in. Experiment, you're not going to blow up your guitar! As you look over the chart, you will see lots of chords you don't know. Either change the song to an easier key or get out your chord book and start learning some new chords.

The above is an extremely simplified and limited explanation of a key. Basically it's just adequate for a beginner. Hey, that's us!

CONFUSING NUMBER ALERT! One of the things that confuses beginners is that numbers can mean so many things. For instance if I say, "play a two", what does that mean? second string? second fret? type 2 power chord? If somebody starts spouting numbers at you, make them slow down and define what those numbers refer to; string, fret, degree, etc.

Tablature:

Tablature is an alternative to standard music notation. It works mainly for guitar and bass. Tablature (tab for short), gives an over head view of the fretboard. Each of the six lines represents a string, and the numbers written on the line tell what frets to play. You read the numbers from left to right, (not top to bottom). Numbers stacked on top of each other mean you play them together. Tab tells you exactly *where* to put your fingers on the guitar neck, it doesn't tell you *what* fingers to use, that's up to you.

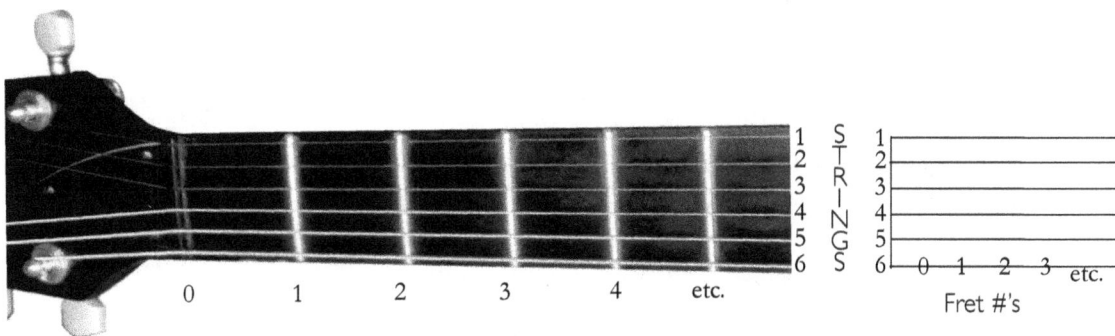

Rhythm Notation:

Rhythm, or strumming, is hard for a lot of people. In fact, many people come to lessons swearing they have no rhythm, (others just swear). This simply isn't true in my experience. If you listen to music for pleasure, you have rhythm, it's just not developed. Luckily if you can read read and understand simple rhythm notation you *will* get the feel. To understand rhythm notation you need to know two things; the *tempo* of the song, and the *time value* of the notes.

- **Tempo:** Whenever you listen to a song, you'll probably find yourself tapping your foot along with it. This steady pulse is called the tempo. In most popular music the beats are arranged in groups of four, (sometimes groups of three), which repeat continuously. These groups of beats are written as a **measure** of music (also called a bar). These measures are separated by lines, called **bar lines.**

All music takes place on this continuous cycle of beats, don't stop!

Track #31
Rhythm Notation
(Example 1)

*The top number of the time signature tells how many beats are grouped in a measure. 4/4 is four beat groups, 3/4 is three beat groups.

- **Notes (time value):** While the tempo may be non-stop, the notes played along with the tempo can be different lengths of time. For simple stuff, we only need four types of notes:

  - **Whole Note:** lasts four beats.
  - **Half Note:** lasts two beats.
  - **Quarter Note:** Gets one beat.
  - **Eighth Note:** gets half beat. The best way to count this note is like P.E. exercises; 1&2&3&4&, etc.

Name	Regular Note	Rhythm Note	Duration (# of beats)	Rest
Whole	○	◇	4	▬
Half	♩ (open)	◇	2	▬
Quarter	♩	⌐	1	𝄽
Eighth	♪	⌐	1/2	𝄾
2 Eighth Notes	♫		Two Eigth notes are connected by a beam	(count: 1 &)

*The shape of a note tells how many beats it gets. Most people find it helpful to count rhythms out loud when they are first learning. To help you, I have put the numbers under each example. Try saying them while you're learning, it really helps.

You can create rhythms by mixing the notes.

Ex.2-A

count: 1   2   3   4   1   2   3   4

*These examples are in rhythm notation, not regular notation.

Track #32
Rhythm Notation
(Example 2)
(Played on 6th String E)

Ex.2-B

count: 1   2   &   3   &   1   2   3

While understanding tempo and recognizing the four main types of notes is enough for simple stuff, you will likely encounter three additional symbols; **rests, ties,** and **dots.** These allow more interesting, (and difficult), rhythms.

• **Rests:** Silence is a big part of music. It is just as important to know when to *stop playing* as it is to play. Silence can be used to intensify the rhythm, or for dramatic effect. In written music, silent periods are written as rests. Each musical note value has its' equivalent rest. A rest tells you not to play for a specific time. *(Refer to the chart above.)*

  *A rest means silence, so you must stop the previous note from playing. (Lift your finger off the note, or touch the string with your pick.) If you continue to let the note ring, you just have a longer note, not a rest.

- **Ties:** The notes we've learned so far limit us quite a bit. How can we play a three beat note, or a five and a half beat note? The possibilities are endless and we can't have a different shape of note for every possible length of time. Luckily the music gods have come to our rescue with a couple of ways to finagle our four basic notes into any length we want. The easiest way is with a tie. A tie is a curved line that links notes of the same pitch together. You simply add up the time values of all the notes tied together into one big note.

Ex.3-A

count:　1 2　3　4　1 2　3　4

(2+1=3 beats)　(2+2=4 beats)

*Never play any notes except the first one under a tie, just keep holding it down for the total time amount under the curved line.

Track #33
Rhythm Notation
(Example 3)
(Played on 6th String E)

Ex.3-B

count:　1　2　3　4　1　2　3　4

(4+2+1=7 beats)

- **Dots:** A dot is placed immediately after any note and adds one half (50%) of that notes' time value, like a tie.

=

count:　1　2　3　count:　1　2　3

(both get three beats)

(the dot adds one beat: 50% of half note)

=

count: 1 2 & 3 4　count: 1 2 & 3 4

(both get one and a half beats)

(the dot adds a half beat: 50% of quarter note)

Strings, Picks, Amps, Etc.:

Strings: It baffles me why so many guitarists ignore their strings. They'll happily shell out thousands of $ for a great guitar and then play on a pathetic set of crusty old strings until one pops. Strings are half your sound! Strings are cheap! Take care of your strings; keep them clean and change them regularly, every month or two. Your guitar will play better, stay in tune better, and sound better. All for five dollars or so every two months, (if you change them yourself). Although there are many options when you buy strings, my advice is to stick with a few basics at first.

- **Buy Local:** Local music stores will give you advice and even put your strings on, for a few extra dollars. Watch and learn! Obviously, if there are no music stores in your area, it will have to be mail-order and internet videos. (I've listed a few at the end of this section.)

- **Get a Decent Brand:** GHS, Ernie Ball, D'Addario, Fender and Gibson, among others, all make a good set of strings for five to ten dollars. Many larger stores have their own own label, made by one of the major string makers, which they sell for less. These can be a good buy.

- **Get the Right Type:** Buy extra light gauge*, round wound strings for both acoustic and electric. Get bronze alloy for acoustic and nickel-steel for electric. While you may eventually settle on different strings, the above specs will get you a cheap, good sounding, easy to play set of strings.

  *Extra light gauge refers to the thickness of your strings. The thinner they are, the easier to play, (too thin and they'll break easy and buzz). The gauge of a string is specified by a number, which is the strings' diameter in fractions of an inch. (.010 means ten thousandths of an inch in diameter.) String sets are named after the diameter of the first string, you don't have to know all the string diameters! For acoustic guitar, extra light strings are called 10's (first string is .010). For electrics, extra light strings are called 9's, (first string is .009). To sum up;

  - Acoustic strings: extra light, bronze alloy, round wound. (ask for 10's)
  - Electric strings: extra light, nickel-steel alloy, round wound. (ask for 9's)

  (**Nylon Strings** are used only on classical style guitars. The neck is wider on classical guitars, and the strings are harder to keep in tune and put on. I do not recommend these guitars for beginners, unless you have exceptionally delicate fingers.)

Changing Strings: It's much easier to learn how to change strings by watching somebody who knows how; a friend, music store clerk, or internet video. With that in mind, I'll limit myself to a few pointers;

- When you take the string out of the pack, you'll see one end has a tiny round piece of metal attached; this is called the *ball-end*.

- Change one string at a time. Look at how the old string was put on and thread the new string through the bridge the same way. For acoustic guitars you have to remove the bridge pin and push the ball end down the hole in the bridge with the pin.

- When the ball-end is firmly seated in the bridge, bring the plain end of the string up to the correct tuning key and thread it through the hole in the post. Wind the string on the inside of the tuner, away from the key. Things work better this way.

Re-tuning the guitar after changing a string is difficult at first, a more experienced player helps a lot. Otherwise, just tighten the string until you get some kind of note, then get out your electronic tuner and keep turning the key slowly until you get the right note.

Picks: I would recommend thin picks with a standard shape at first; they're easier on your wrist. Later on, when you know what you want, you can experiment. Picks are cheap, so you can't screw up too bad.

Amplifiers: At the beginning stage, you want fairly small and cheap. You won't be playing on stage any time soon. $100, maybe a little less, will get you a five to ten watt* amp with a six inch to ten inch speaker. While more is generally better,(more watts, bigger speaker), quality and actual sound count the most. Peavey, Crate, Fender, and Line 6, among others, all make make good, inexpensive amps.

*watts are how an amps' power is measured, more watts equals more power.

Testing the Amp: Turn on the amp (with the distortion off, and without any cable plugged in at first). Turn up the volume about half way and listen for any loud humming or hissing (not good). Now turn the volume back down and plug in your guitar. Turn the knobs. Do they feel solid and well built, or cheap and cheesy? Do they crackle? (Also not good). Ask the salesman how to get distortion, the heavy rock crunch we all love, if that's important to you. In fact if you don't understand anything about your amp, ask. Write down the answers if you have to. It's much easier to pry information out of that salesman before he gets his hands on your dough!

Tuning:

Using an electronic tuner is best to start. While the old fashioned way of tuning by ear is ultimately better (you don't want to have to use a machine,) modern tuners are a lot easier and more accurate. Nowadays, they're almost as cheap as the old standbys of tuning by ear (the pitch-pipe and tuning fork,) so I would definitely recommend *buy electric!* Tuner that is.

- **Buy an Electric Tuner:** Electronic tuners cost as little as $15.00, and about $20.00 to $25.00 is reasonable for a decent one. Again, buy from a store! Its worth a couple of extra dollars to have a salesman show you how to use it and to have a place to take it back in case it doesn't work. Make sure the tuner works on both acoustic and electric guitars.

- **Using an Electric Tuner:** They're all a little different and they all come with instructions, so *read the instructions!* However, I do have a few hints that will help on most tuners.

    1. Make sure your guitar is in tune when you leave the store! A tuner has to have something to work with. If the strings are flopping off the neck, your poor tuner can't tell you anything. If the guitar is reasonably in tune, and you don't drop it or mess with the keys you should be okay.

    2. Pick firmly and keep picking! Don't let the note fade out (and electric players, turn up the volume on the guitar!)

    3. Turn the key slowly and watch the meter, you should be able to see the pitch go up and down. You *are* on the right string aren't you?

    4. When you've tuned all six strings, go back and re-check your tuning. Sometimes your guitar will shift a little and you might have to touch it up. It should *not* take more than one turn of your key in either direction to bring your string in tune. If you can't get it in tune, find someone who can (and find out why it got that far out of tune). Don't pop the string.

Standard Tuning: This is how tuning was taught in the "old days" before tuners. It requires a pretty good musical ear, so if you can't get it, use a tuner. Ready?

- **Get a Source of Pitch:** I would recommend **pitch-pipe**; a tuning fork is too difficult for a beginner. Make sure you get a pitch pipe for guitar, not some other instrument. You will notice you have six pipes, one for each string. When you are trying to match the pipe with the string, I find it easier if I press on the 12th fret, instead of trying to match it to the open string; it's the same pitch and easier to hear.

In order to pick the string, turn the key, *and* blow into the pitch pipe, you will have to hold the pitch pipe between your teeth. It looks kind of stupid and you will probably drool a little (ready for a tuner yet?).

Tuning the Guitar to Itself: Many people find it hard to tune to a pitch pipe, the difference in sound between a pipe and a string is just too much. It is possible to tune the guitar without a pitch pipe, by tuning strings to one another.

- Match the 6th string to a source of pitch, (yes you do have to use the pitch pipe, but only once).*

- Press on the 5th fret, 6th string and match the open 5th string to it (both notes should sound the same).

- Press on the 5th fret, 5th string and match open 4th string to it.

- Press on the 5th fret, 4th string and match the open 3rd string to it.

- Press on the 4th fret, 3rd string and match open 2nd string to it.

- Press on the 5th fret, 2nd string and match open 1st string to it.

A Couple of Hints:

- Hum the notes as you play, and listen to your voice, does it go up or down? Don't get fooled by tone differences.

- When you play two notes together that are out of tune, they sound "rough." Keep tuning until the two notes "smooth out."

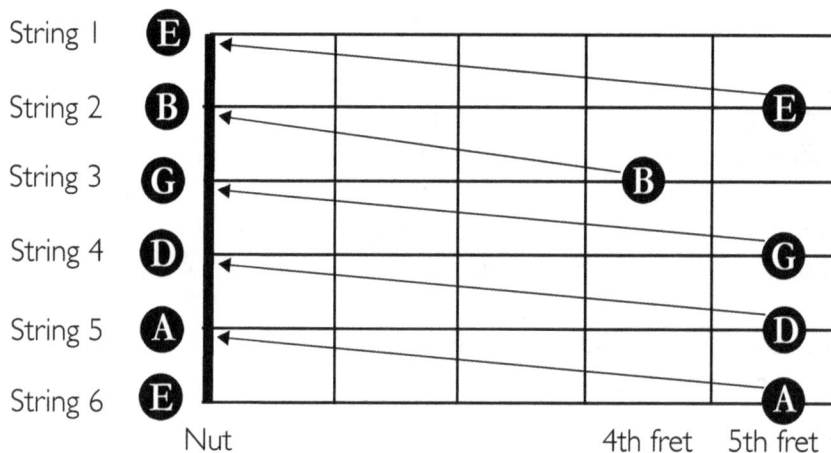

String 1 E
String 2 B   E
String 3 G   B
String 4 D   G
String 5 A   D
String 6 E   A
          Nut   4th fret   5th fret

*If you don't use a pitch-pipe, the guitar will be in tune with itself (but not with anything else on the planet).

Further Resources:

Magazines:

- **Guitar Player** (guitarplayer.com)
- **Guitar World** (guitarworlddigital.com)
- **Acoustic Guitar** (acguitar.com)
- **Total Guitar** (totalguitar.com)
- **Play Guitar Magazine** (playguitarmagazine.com)
- **Guitar Magazine**

Music Stores (online and mail order):

- **Musician's Friend**
  musciansfriend.com
  1866-462-9293

- **Sam Ash**
  samash.com
  1800-472-6274

- **Sweetwater**
  sweetwater.com
  1800-222-4700

- **Music 123**
  music123.com
  1888-566-6123

- **Music 44 (sheet music)**
  music44.com
  1866-419-6497

Tab Sites:

- ultimate-guitar.com
- mxtabs.net
- thetabworld.com
- (or you can type "guitar tabs + song title" into your search engine of choice)